tea for you

tea for you

Blending Custom Teas to Savor and Share

Tracy Stern

Clarkson Potter/Publishers
New York

Library of Congress
Cataloging-in-Publication Data
Stern, Tracy (Tracy Gilbert)
    Tea for you / Tracy Stern. — 1st ed.
        p.   cm.
    Includes index.
    1. Tea.   2. Cookery (Tea).   I. Title.
    TX817.T3S745   2009
    641.3'372—dc22   2008036993

ISBN 978-0-307-45080-7

Printed in China

DESIGN BY JENNIFER K. BEAL DAVIS

10 9 8 7 6 5 4 3 2 1

First Edition

This book is
dedicated to The Artist,
The Musician, The Society Hostess,
The Fashionable Dandy, The Writer,
The Romantic, and The Lover.

And to Chloe Willow and Hunter,
my two angels.

Contents

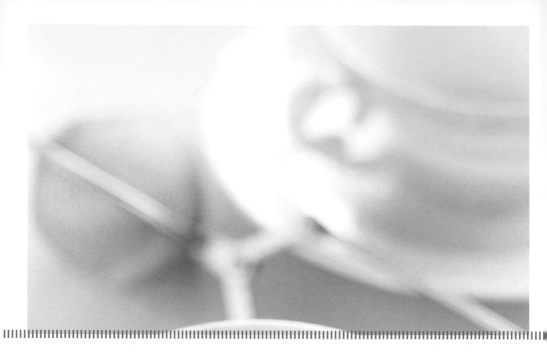

Introduction

It's high time to think outside the teabag. The typical teabag contains
tiny scraps of tea leaves, usually with the flavor equivalent of sawdust. Yes,
it's convenient, but so is instant coffee, and when was the last time you served
that to your family and friends? What's more, brewing a great pot of tea is
even easier than making coffee from scratch and is a lovely ritual to share.

Once you enjoy a superior cup of tea brewed from whole leaves, which
are not only incredibly perfumed but often beautifully flecked with various
ingredients, you'll have a hard time going back to a bagged industrial blend.
And once you have embraced whole leaves, you will probably find that you
already have the makings of a great personalized tea in your home. So why
accept someone else's blend when you can create tea for you?

In this book, I will share the expert secrets I have learned from years of
mingling the finest ingredients to craft my signature tea blends. You will
learn how to create a special, playful "house blend" that no one can taste
anywhere but in your home, and how to pair teas, spices, herbs, and other
natural botanicals to dream up one-of-a-kind teas to give as gifts. For that
someone in your life who adores chocolate, you might choose a black tea
with Assam leaves from India and mix in unsweetened cocoa powder and
fragrant vanilla bean. For a friend with a weak spot for jasmine tea, a blend
of green tea with extra jasmine and chopped dried apple might be just the
right combination. What could be more thoughtful than warming a loved
one's heart with a homemade tea that flaunts her favorite flavors?

Blending teas is easy. All you have to do is figure out what flavors you like
best. I will introduce you to the basics, including the flavor profiles of the wide
array of natural ingredients you will have to choose from for inspiration.
Once you've determined your favorite combinations, there simply will be no
limit to your creativity and you will be on your way to making tea for you!

··· introduction ···

9

Tea Basics

All artists start with a firm grounding in the classics and traditions of their craft. And so, before plunging into the specifics of flavors and aromas of the array of ingredients in the tea blender's pantry, let's begin with some fundamentals of tea itself: its origins, how it is processed, the marvelous health benefits associated with various teas, how to buy and store tea, and how to brew the perfect cup.

Tea Origins

All tea leaves come from a warm-weather evergreen plant called *Camellia sinensis*. Teas come from all over the world. Most take their names from the district in which they are grown, as do many wines and certain cheeses. Much of the world's tea comes from mountainous regions, up to 7,000 feet above sea level. The leading producers of tea are China, India, Argentina, Brazil, Kenya, Indonesia, Tanzania, Sri Lanka, and Malawi.

When the leaves are harvested (at varying maturity levels), what happens to them next, the way they are processed, and the amount of oxygen they are exposed to—a process called oxidation (also called fermentation)—all determine what kind of tea will result: white, green, oolong, or black.

Tea contains certain enzymes that interact with oxygen when the tea leaf is broken or crushed. When the leaf is heated until it dries, the oxidation stops. Nothing is added to the tea leaves, but water is taken away during processing. Tea leaves go from freshly plucked, steamed, sun-withered, or roasted; then they are rolled and graded. The process takes approximately sixteen hours. During the processing, the removal of all moisture changes the leaf's texture. The reasons for drying tea are for color enhancement, aroma, and stabilization. After processing, the tea will keep for approximately two years.

How Tea Is Made

Most tea plants or bushes yield more than a thousand tea leaves every year, which may seem like a lot until you realize that it takes more than two thousand leaves to produce a pound of fully processed tea. And those leaves are harvested either by hand or by mechanized techniques. If the leaves are gathered manually, workers procure the top two leaves and the bud from each branch of the plant. In the finest tea estates, the workers wear white gloves to ensure that the natural oils in the roller's skin does not come into contact with the leaves, thus protecting the purity of each and every leaf. Due to the tremendous demand for tea, many harvesters rely on machinery to gather tea leaves, and while this may in the end reduce the quality of the tea, it certainly reduces expenses. Connoisseurs tend to seek out hand-harvested tea leaves.

White and green tea leaves undergo very little processing and no oxidation, or fermentation. White tea is harvested before the leaves are all the way open, when the buds are still covered with the fine white fur that gives the tea its name. White tea has a light, almost sweet flavor, while green tea is famously grassy. **Oolong tea** is only partially oxidized, for two to three hours, whereas **black tea** is oxidized for up to four hours. The result is the bold and hearty flavor that makes black tea by far the most popular tea in America.

In processing all teas, the step that halts fermentation is called firing. Leaves are placed in large hot pans to lose nearly all of their original moisture. The length of time required to dry the leaves varies according to the freshness of the leaves and the length of time the leaves have fermented. Obviously, this important step must be done carefully, or the tea will lose its flavor and may even spoil and crumble. Under modern circumstances, firing is done in a large special dryer that can maintain a constant temperature of 120 degrees. Once leaves are heated and dried, the process of fermentation stops.

After tea is processed, the leaves are sorted by size so that they'll brew evenly. The highest quality (and most expensive) tea usually comes from

whole leaves. The grading of tea leaves for consumers is a fairly confusing process, in part because there are different grading procedures for green and black teas, and the procedures vary by country. Grades refer not to the tea's flavor, but rather to the size of the leaves and how the leaves were processed. Whole tea leaves are awarded the highest grades because they're more difficult to produce. Because tea is primarily processed in cultures where nothing is wasted, dust (also called fannings) from the leaves tends to end up in commercial tea bags. The dust makes for a murky, muddled cup of brewed tea that sings mainly one overly loud note. Excellent-quality whole-leaf teas produce a refined brew with a harmonious symphony of flavors.

Tea and Health

The health benefits of drinking tea have been well documented. Tea has been shown to prime the body's immune system to fight infection and actually prevent the onset of many illnesses. Tea contains naturally occurring compounds called flavonoids, which are believed to have antioxidant characteristics. Antioxidants are celebrated for helping to neutralize free radicals, which can damage various essential physical elements, including lipids (essential fatty acids) and genetic material.

Studies indicate that antioxidant properties in tea can help minimize the risk of developing stomach and other types of cancer, and that drinking one cup of tea a day could reduce heart attack risk by up to 50 percent! A risk reduction in the incidence of skin cancer among tea drinkers has been identified; two research projects found that tea-drinking women attained higher bone density measurements than those who are not tea drinkers.

Research has shown similar results for drinkers of both green and black tea, though the health benefits of green tea seem to be emerging more impressively with each passing day.

Of course tea has no fat or cholesterol, sodium, or sugar. It is free of calories. Tea consumption helps to maintain proper fluid balance. And quantities consumed daily can definitely be an important factor in your health—drinking three to five cups of tea per day can provide what scientists have described as significant heart health benefits. One study, published in the *American Journal of Clinical Nutrition* in 2002, showed that people who drank more than three cups of black tea per day reduced their risk of heart attack by 43 percent compared with non–tea drinkers. And the United States Department of Agriculture conducted a study in 2003 that showed that people who drank five cups of black tea every day and moderated their fat and cholesterol intake were able to reduce their LDL (or "bad") cholesterol levels by about 11 percent after just three weeks!

White tea seems to help prevent skin from aging and also has antiviral *and* antibacterial properties.

Green tea has been shown to contain fluoride, which helps to prevent cavities and wipes out bacteria in the mouth to combat bad breath. Perhaps more important, the fluoride in green tea helps to protect against arterial sclerosis, or hardening of the arteries, by obstructing the oxidation of cholesterol in the bloodstream.

White, green, oolong, and black tea contain caffeine in increasing degrees: the longer the tea leaves have fermented, the higher their caffeine level will be. Additionally, the longer the brewing time, the more caffeine will end up in a serving. White tea has 5 to 15 milligrams of caffeine per serving, while green has 8 to 16 milligrams (which is far less than most caffeinated sodas), oolong has 12 to 55, and black has 25 to 110. (A cup of brewed black coffee has between 80 and 135 milligrams of caffeine.) Tea brewed from whole leaves will result in about half the caffeine of that brewed from a tea bag; since the leaves are all chopped up in the latter, more tea-leaf surface area is exposed to the hot water.

Herbal and botanical teas are utterly caffeine-free. While the potential health benefits linked to traditional teas do not apply to herbal teas, the unique ingredients in them—flowers, leaves, bark, seeds, and roots of all kinds from other plants—are often associated with their own health properties. Spices, in particular, have been revered since ancient times for their healing and health-promoting qualities.

Buying and Storing Tea

Most of the ingredients mentioned in this book are available in a well-stocked supermarket as well as in tea shops, large health food stores, gourmet spice shops, and online. I've provided the addresses of my favorite Internet sites in the Resources section (see page 93). Try to find whole-leaf teas, or OP (orange pekoe), the grade for whole leaves. Good tea dealers—and savvy Web sites—will steer you toward these grades.

Tea should always be stored in an airtight container away from light, heat, and moisture. Because all heat rises, store your tea in a low cupboard instead of one overhead. Never refrigerate or freeze tea leaves. And unless you're a real tea fiend, don't buy tea in huge quantities. After its package or container has been opened for the first time, tea, like many dried herbs, slowly begins to lose its flavor. Tea should be used within six months of opening.

If you're giving tea as a gift, keep in mind that tea should always be kept in a cool dry place, but that gives you plenty of leeway in terms of gift presentation. For ideas, I like to hit the local five-and-dime store, as well as museum gift shops and stationery stores. Mason jars or acrylic boxes work nicely; I love to see how beautiful the teas are. You can wrap the lid of a jar with fabric or paper and include a recipe. If you use an old or new tin, you can always put the tea in a plastic bag inside the tin. Silver or porcelain sugar jars with lids can be found at flea markets or garage sales. Fancy mailing envelopes can be filled with tea and tied with string; colorful cellophane bags can be filled and tied with ribbon. You can make tea blends for children's classes, or as a goodie bag at a charity event. A bath tea blend makes the perfect gift for a friend who just came home from the hospital. In late spring, give someone dear to you a bowl of lemons with some black tea so they can have a summer of lemon iced tea.

The Perfect Cup

Brewing a wonderful cup of tea is hardly rocket science, but there are some important tips to keep in mind for superior results:

You'll need a **tea kettle** or saucepan to boil the water and a **teapot** to brew the tea and serve it attractively. Many teapots have a strainer at the base of their spout or come with a tea-infusing insert. If not, I recommend purchasing a **tea diffuser or tea ball** to hold the tea leaves. Using a diffuser or tea filter gives you a lot more control over the strength of the tea, because you can remove it as soon as the tea looks done to your liking, instead of letting loose leaves continue to brew in the pot until the last cup of tea is served. I've also used a fairly new product, paper tea filters, which have a top flap that is lifted to measure the tea into an expanding pouch. The brand I've used is made by Finum in Germany, and the filters are made of abaca pulp, cellulose, and sealing fiber. They're unbleached and biode-gradable and available at specialty tea shops around the country. If all of these choices are unavailable, you can always strain the tea leaves from the tea before serving, but this can be a little inelegant when done at the table.

It is traditional to warm the teapot so your tea brews at the proper temperature and does not cool down too quickly while steeping: pour a little boiling or very hot water into the pot, swirl it around, let the pot sit for 10 seconds, and then pour out the water.

Because so many tea flavors are delicate, it's a good idea to use **well-filtered or bottled spring water** instead of tap water, which so often contains protective chemicals. If using tap, always start with cold water, not hot. Never use previously boiled or distilled water, which can flatten flavors. Black, oolong, and herbal teas should be brewed with water brought to a rolling boil over medium-high heat. White and green teas, however, should not be made with boiling water, because the high heat can bring out a bitterness in the delicate leaves. Bring water to a boil, turn off the heat, and then let the water cool for a few minutes before using.

For the **tea** itself, add one level teaspoon (about 2 grams) of tea "for the pot," and one teaspoon per cup of water used. Most green and white teas are

ready in two to three minutes, while black and herbal teas need a bit longer, four to five minutes. If you like your tea strong, steeping it longer than recommended is not the solution. Oversteeping results in bitter and abrasive tea. Simply use more tea and steep it as directed, instead. When you've reached the recommended steeping time, remove the infuser, pour the tea into a cup, and enjoy the aroma and flavors of your tea while it's nice and hot. This is essentially the British method of brewing tea, and it is favored by most tea lovers in America. Some cultures, such as those in Turkey and Russia and parts of India, actually prepare a strong and concentrated tea, then dilute it with hot water for every new cup as needed.

To make iced tea, follow the same instructions for making hot tea, but use two level teaspoons (4 grams) of tea per cup. After it's brewed to the proper strength, as above, remove the tea infuser and let the tea cool to room temperature. Serve in tumblers with plenty of ice.

Sun tea—tea made in a large pitcher left in sunlight for a few hours—can harbor dangerous bacteria. Tea steeped in a jar on a sunny window ledge or on a porch won't get any warmer than 130 degrees—no warmer than a hot bath, and not nearly hot enough to kill bacteria that may be lurking in the water or in the tea itself. Such germs are killed only in water that has been heated to 195 degrees for five minutes. Caffeine will help prevent bacteria from growing for a few hours, but that's it. Herbal teas are even riskier because they have no caffeine at all.

If you really want sun tea—and some aficionados feel that it lacks any bitterness that can result in tea made with boiling water—make sure that you use a very clean container. If the container has a spout, take extra care to keep it sparkling clean. Don't brew tea in the sun for more than three hours, and don't make more tea than you plan to drink on the same day. Refrigerate the tea as soon as it's ready and keep it cold. Or better yet, brew the tea right in the refrigerator. You really don't need the sun at all—that's an old wives' tale! Fill a pitcher with four cups of cold water, add four to six teaspoons of tea, and refrigerate it for six hours or even overnight.

Serving Tea

There are certain rules of thumb involved in choosing teas for different times of the day. Breakfast tea should be strong and dark. English breakfast tea is a mix of different black teas to jump-start your day. Personally, I love chai tea for breakfast. It's the best tea to brew if you're trying to break your coffee habit. It begins with strong Assam tea from India that has been withered into black tea with a malty flavor. To that brew you add milk or cream and honey or sugar, with spices like cardamom, cinnamon, cloves, ginger, and even black pepper. That combination will certainly wake you up and you'll forget that coffee ever existed.

For lunch, I drink clean green or white tea to complement my fare, usually a light salad or sushi. Later in the afternoon, I like to have a dose of green or white tea as a pick-me-up. After dinner, it's best to go with either a decaffeinated tea or a fruity, spicy herbal tea, such as rooibos. To put me to sleep, I make an herbal tea of lavender and chamomile. If I need to stay awake to write or socialize, I have a sweet, spicy chocolate chai with caffeine. Mixing and matching different teas with all their different healthy properties can be like taking your daily vitamins.

Flavor Profiles of Teas, Spices, Herbs, and Botanicals

The flavors and fragrances of teas and their blending ingredients are many and highly varied in potency. Their interactions can be sweeping and heady, or very subtle and alluring. It's amazing how many ways the various ingredients can arouse one another's flavors and aromas, and seduce your senses in the process. No wonder some cultures regard certain tea blends as aphrodisiacs!

We'll discuss which ingredients marry well with which teas in the following chapter, but let's start by exploring the flavors in some of the most commonly found teas and tea ingredients.

Traditional Teas

When you start blending your own teas, these teas will serve as your base ingredients for caffeinated brews, setting the framework for the final tea and often determining the direction, be it strong or subtle.

Assam tea, an Indian black tea, has an assertive, slightly malty flavor and is considered a fine breakfast tea due to its brisk wake-me-up flavor and bright color. It brews up to a dark reddish mahogany color, and it goes well with milk or lemon.

Black tea is the most common of all teas. It is usually flavored and scented with spices, oils, and/or flower petals, so the flavor of the tea can vary, as can the actual name of the tea (Assam, for example, is a black tea). Regular black tea is among the highest in caffeine, though if not brewed too long, it still has less caffeine than coffee.

Ceylon tea comes, of course, from Ceylon, called Sri Lanka since 1972. It's a black tea with distinctly citric notes, but the flavor can vary because it's grown in numerous areas of Sri Lanka. It usually tastes strong with lemony notes, and its brewed color is reddish amber.

Chai is an Indian spiced black tea blend, usually featuring cinnamon, ginger, cardamom, cloves, and black peppercorns. It is famously spicy and complex, and is usually reddish brown when brewed. It is often served sweetened and lightened with milk.

Darjeeling tea, from the Darjeeling area of West Bengal, India, is one of the finest grades of tea. It has a pungent, floral aroma and a certain tannic spiciness. Some people think it smells like wine. Younger leaves harvested in early spring produce fragrant light brewed tea sold as "first flush." The second harvest in summer is more full-bodied. Leaves harvested in the fall are usually very mild. Most Darjeeling teas brew up to a soft amber color. The flavors are so special that the tea is usually not served with milk.

Earl Grey is a black tea that is flavored and scented with oil from the rind of sour bergamot oranges, the same oil that is found in many women's *and* men's perfumes. It is indeed quite fragrant and exotic, and it brews to a reddish brown.

English breakfast is a blend of Indian black teas that is so assertively flavored and tangy that many prefer to tame it with milk and/or sugar or honey. It brews up to a deep brown.

Formosa oolong is from Taiwan. Because it's only partly fermented, its flavor starts out very subtly, but there's a bit of a bite waiting. It has the rich flavor of black tea and the light tanginess of green tea. Often, oolong is blended with flower petals or herbs. It brews to a yellow-green color.

Chai

Silver Needles

Gunpowder

Genmaicha

Oolong

Green tea is gaining in popularity by leaps and bounds, due to its celebrated healthful properties and refreshing grassy flavor. It is favored by people who prefer less caffeine, but still want a little kick of it. Because it is minimally processed, many of the original and wonderful properties of the tea leaf remain. Generally, Chinese green tea is more strongly flavored than Japanese green tea, because Chinese tea leaves are usually pan-fried or roasted, while Japanese are processed with steam. By all means, try both!

Genmaicha is a Japanese green tea, sencha, that is stirred with puffed brown rice kernels to give it a smoky taste. It has a very light, nutty flavor and the aroma of popcorn. It brews up to be pale green and sometimes cloudy.

Gunpowder is a green tea from China. The leaves are rolled up into little pellets. The tea is quite strong with a roasted aroma. It brews to dark gold.

Hojicha is a Japanese green tea. It has toasty and nutlike flavors, and unlike most green teas, it brews to a golden brown.

Irish breakfast is a blend of Assam and Ceylon black teas. As such, it's quite hearty and a little more tart than English breakfast. Its brewed color is deep reddened brown.

Keemun is a black tea from southwestern China. Its mellow, light-hearted flavor is strong, and a little on the sweet side with smoky notes. It steeps to a reddish brown.

Chinese Green Tea

Darjeeling

Matcha

Jasmine tea is a black tea blended with dried jasmine flowers. It's quite floral, aromatic, and almost sweet, and it brews to a light reddish brown.

Lapsang souchong is a smoked black tea that originated in the Fujian Province of China. The tea leaves are semidried over cedar or pine fires, then pan fired and oxidized, and finally spread out in bamboo baskets suspended over burning pine or cedar to dry out fully. Obviously, the tea tastes very smoky. It brews to a dark brown.

Lung ching is a Chinese green tea with creamy and nutlike flavors. When brewed, it is pale gold.

Mao feng, a green tea from southeastern China, is notably brisk and a little sweet. It brews to light gold with green tinges.

Masala chai is a blend of strong Indian black tea with so-called warm spices (masala is the Indian word for spice blend) including cinnamon, cardamom, ginger, cloves, black pepper, star anise, and sometimes nutmeg, cocoa, licorice, vanilla, or even saffron. It is frequently served with milk and sugar or honey. In addition to its beguiling depth of flavor, the chai plant has the highest levels of omega-3 in any plant on the planet.

Matcha is a Japanese powdered green tea used to dye and flavor foods like soba noodles and green tea ice cream. It has a light sweetness not found in other green tea and brews to pale green.

Nilgiri is grown in southern India. It's a very dark black tea with a flowery fragrance. It brews into a brisk, medium-bodied tea with very little, if any, of the astringency that most black teas have. It brews to a deep copper color.

Oolong is a Chinese tea that is oxidized to a level somewhere between black and green tea, or 10 to 70 percent oxidation. It is the most complex tea and tastes more like green tea than black, but without the strong grassiness and with more nuances. Flavors range from floral to earthy and sweet.

Orange pekoe is not an orange-flavored tea. Rather it is a term used in the tea industry to refer to a high-grade black tea that features large pieces of leaves or even whole leaves.

Pi lo chun is a green tea from Taiwan and China. Its fruitlike flavors, especially apricot, have made it very popular. It is pale amber when brewed.

Pouchong is an oolong tea from Taiwan. It has an almost startlingly earthy flavor. When fully brewed it's only light green.

Pu'er is an oolong tea from southwestern China. It has rough-and-tumble musty flavors and brews to a very dark brown.

Russian caravan is a blend of Indian and Chinese black teas, often including the famously smoky lapsang souchong. It is intensely flavored, with a darkly smoky taste.

Sencha is a very popular Japanese green tea, with a refreshing and pleasant flavor. It brews only to a very pale green.

Sikkim is a black tea from northeastern India. It has a delicate, slightly malty flavor and brews only to a yellow amber color.

Silver needles is a white tea from Fujian, China. It has nutty, almost sweet flavors and brews to a pale ochre.

Ti Kwan Yin, an oolong tea from Taiwan and China, has a soft floral aroma and creamy and complex flavors. The finished brew is amber yellow.

White Darjeeling is a white tea from northeastern India. It has mellow, lightly lemony flavors and pale amber color.

White tea comes mostly from China and is harvested from the first buds of the tea plant. It is very lightly flavored, with herbal and mineral notes. It's also quite fragrant, and it's the lowest in caffeine of any tea.

White peony is a white tea from Fujian, China. It's quite delicate and satiny, making a drink with a pale gold color.

Wu Yi is an oolong tea from the Wu Yi Mountains in southeastern China. It has a robust but civilized flavor and is reddish amber.

Yunnan is a black tea from southwestern China. It has rich peppery flavors and is favored by those who like strong brews. Even its color when brewed, a deep reddened brown, is darker than that of most teas.

Hibiscus

Rooibos

Lavender

Chamomile

Yerba Maté

Herbal Teas

These herbal and floral ingredients, once dried, are often used solo to make noncaffeinated teas. Think of them, too, as candidates for blending.

Chamomile comes from the sunflower family. Chamomile tea is made from German chamomile buds, which grow all over the world. It has a soft, smooth, earthy flavor and a strong, flowery, haylike aroma, which has made it very popular with aromatherapists and herbologists. It is also well known for its calming and anti-inflammatory properties, and it has a long history of being involved in resolving such skin disorders as acne, rashes, psoriasis, and eczema. The tea brews to a light gold.

Hibiscus tea, which brews to a bright red color, has been associated with lowering blood pressure and cholesterol, while enhancing energy levels. In countries with warmer climates, especially Africa and Mexico, hibiscus tea is well known for its cooling qualities. It is also rich in vitamin C. Hibiscus petals lend a lightly tart cranberry flavor to tea blends and can be found in many Hispanic markets.

Lavender makes for a relatively strong-flavored tea and must be used sparingly to avoid a soapy flavor. Lavender has been shown to ease stress, soothe jitters, and even relieve mild depression. It's also wonderful for easing headaches. It has anti-inflammatory and disinfectant properties, and it can soothe the effects of insect bites. A cup of hot water infused with lavender has been shown to help induce sleep. When diluted with water or witch hazel, lavender oil can help to heal acne.

Lemon verbena is a full-bodied herb with a strong lemon fragrance and flavor. The brewed tea is pale yellow. It is favored in Europe for making relaxing, digestive after-dinner tisanes.

Peppermint tea is made from cut-leaf peppermint. Depending on the amount used and the brewing time, the tea can be faintly minty or very strong, almost like a breath mint. Mint tea can be made from any variety of the herb, fresh or dried. Use dried for blending, however. Depending on the length of the brew, peppermint tea brews to a pale or medium green.

Rooibos, or red tea, tastes rather like black tea but isn't really tea at all. It's made from an herb found only in South Africa. It is harvested manually from *Aspalathus linearis,* a plant that is indigenous to the country. The leaves remain green until they are fermented in mounds, then spread out to dry in sunlight, when the leaves turn red. Red tea has 400 percent more nutrients than regular tea. It tastes piney and earthy and earns its name by brewing up crimson.

Yerba maté is a green herbal tea popular in Latin America. It has quite bitter flavors and is dark amber when brewed up.

More Tea Ingredients

Here are some of the herbs, spices, and other flavorings I use most commonly in my tea blends. If a caffeinated tea or herbal tea is your primary note, these ingredients can add tantalizing aromas and tastes to round out a subtly or robustly flavored brew. This list is by no means exhaustive but is a good place to begin as you identify your favorite flavors. It's time to let your personal preferences stand out.

It is worth noting that when you use fruit peels, herbs, and spices, it is a good idea to seek out organic or—in the case of flowers and petals—unsprayed products to avoid pesticides for health reasons and also for best flavor. For herbs, you can use them fresh if you're brewing a tea right away, or dried if you're making a tea to give or store in your cupboard. For spices, you can opt for the whole spice or for ground, the flavor of which is a bit muted.

Almond extract is a pungent flavoring made by combining bitter almond oil with ethyl alcohol. It should be used sparingly and carefully. I sprinkle a little on tea leaves in a roomy jar, cover and shake the jar, and let the mixture rest overnight before brewing tea. I sometimes crush up some roasted almonds and add them to the tea blend, too. Toasted nuts have much more flavor than plain raw ones.

Cacao comes from a tropical evergreen tree cultivated for its seeds. The seeds are used to make cocoa powder, cocoa butter, and of course chocolate. I use crushed cacao seeds, called nibs or bits, which impart flavor but not really color, and also real chocolate shavings in my teas.

Cardamom is a member of the ginger family, native to India. The seeds are encased in a pod about the size of a tiny grape, with about twenty seeds per pod. The seeds are ground to a powder that has a sweet and spicy flavor.

Cassis is a European black currant that, when dried, gives tea a delightful berry flavor.

Cinnamon is the inner bark of a tropical evergreen tree. The bark dries into a curled quill, which is chopped into finger-length pieces and sold as sticks, or is ground into a fine powder. The flavor is slightly bittersweet.

Citrus zest, or fruit peel, is a very popular tea and herbal tea flavoring. Citrus fruit with tight skin—not bumpy or pocked—will have more citrus oil in the skin, and therefore more flavor. Even if you're using organic fruit, wash and dry it thoroughly, and cut out any bad spots or discolorations.

Cardamom

Cinnamon

Peppercorns

Orange Peel

Star Anise

Using a vegetable peeler or knife, cut the zest from the fruit, using a sawing motion. You want as little of the pith (the white flesh under the zest) as possible, because it is very bitter. Let the strips air-dry for four to five days until brittle. Store them in a small covered jar. You can either chop or grind the peels to release the stored citrus oil, and use them in your tea or herbal tea blends. Start out by using the zest sparingly—it can easily overwhelm many other flavors. Citrus zest is among the most bracing additions to any tea blend.

Cloves are the dried unopened bud of the evergreen clove tree. Their powerful cinnamon-like flavor means they should be used sparingly in tea.

Coconut flakes are the dried shredded meat of coconuts and are available sweetened or unsweetened. The flakes have a tropical, exotic, slightly soapy flavor.

Dehydrated or freeze-dried fruits are widely available and can be grated and used in tea blends. You can't get the low moisture content needed for long-term storage by drying fruits at home, so stick with store-bought, preferably organic. Certain dehydrated fruits, such as dried banana and apricot, have fairly overpowering flavor and should be used sparingly in tea blends. Apple, mango, cherry, and other fruits should definitely be explored.

Goji berries are bright red and not as sweet as raisins, but not as tart as cranberries. They're known as the antiaging berry and are sold dried.

Ginger is invigoratingly spicy and can help ward off a cold. I prefer to use it fresh in a tea ball, and I let it steep for fifteen minutes.

Jasmine flowers and oil are used in perfumes, as well as in food and tea flavorings. The aroma and flavor are floral and slightly sweet.

Lemongrass is very important in Thai and Vietnamese cookery. It has long, thin, green-gray leaves and a scallionlike bulbous base. It has a pungent sour lemon flavor.

Nutmeg, when whole, is egg shaped and about ½ to 1 inch long. Don't bother with preground nutmeg. The scent and flavor of freshly ground or grated nutmeg is warm and spicy.

Orange-tree blossoms are dried and used to make tea in Spain. They are aromatic and lend a very subtle and delicately citric flavor to tea.

Peppercorns add spice to tea blends. The strongest available, black peppercorns are picked before they are quite ripe, then dried until the skin turns black. White peppercorns are those that have been allowed to ripen, then the skin is removed and the berry is dried. Green peppercorns are underripe and are less pungent than the others. Actually dried berries and not true peppercorns, pink peppercorns add color and a delicate flavor to teas.

Rose hips are usually red to orange, but they may be purple and even black. They are the fruit of roses and have a pungent sour flavor. They are a wonderful source of vitamin C and as such are often dried and ground to be sold in health food stores in powder or tablet form.

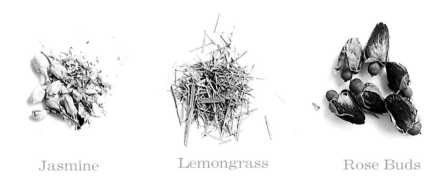

Jasmine   Lemongrass   Rose Buds

Rose petals have an affinity for the heart. Like lavender and chamomile, rose petals are incredibly fragrant and have anti-inflammatory properties. Rose oil can help relieve irritability and muscle cramps associated with menstruation. The oil's rehydrating capabilities make it useful for dry skin and various rashes. Like lavender, it should be used in moderation in tea blends to avoid creating a soapy aftertaste.

Rosemary is a Mediterranean herb with needle-shaped leaves that taste piney and lemony.

Sage is a strong piney herb with a rich history as a medicinal tea, used to treat sore throats. It has licorice notes and is familiar to anyone who has eaten breakfast sausages. Its brew reaches a yellow-green color.

Star anise is a beautiful dried, star-shaped spice that tastes like licorice.

Tarragon has long, narrow, tender leaves with light licorice flavor. It should be used sparingly because it can easily dominate other flavors.

Thyme is a member of the mint family. Its tiny leaves have a strong, minty, light-lemony flavor.

Vanilla beans were originally used by the Aztecs to augment the flavor of chocolate, and they still do a fine job of that today; I usually use vanilla with some form of chocolate in my teas. The narrow, dark pods contain thousands of highly aromatic tiny seeds packed with irresistible flavor.

Creating Your Own
Tea Blends

Becoming your own mix master is easy! Once you have a passing familiarity with the ingredients at hand, and you learn to trust and follow your taste, there are no mistakes. Above all, have fun with your blending. Even kids can come up with some wonderful and often highly creative blends.

Every time I develop a new tea blend, I imagine a personality—or better, an actual person—for whom to make the blend. When I dreamed up the signature teas in my SALONTEA line, I began by trying to envision the kinds of characters who would come to an eighteenth-century tea salon for afternoon tea. When I created one of my most popular blends, The Lover, I thought about the ultimate lovers' holiday, Valentine's Day. And we all know no Valentine's Day would be complete without chocolate! I envisioned an eighteenth-century woman of a certain standing, but not a woman above romantic dalliances. I know how much women love chocolate and vanilla (well, I certainly do!), so I made a seductive blend of fine bits of cacao and vanilla beans and blended them with a special chai tea made from an Assam tea with cinnamon, cardamom, and clove. Cinnamon stimulates the aromas and flavors of the other spices, making them work their magic more quickly. The Lover blend is a natural and spicy aphrodisiac that energizes while it seduces.

For The Musician, I wanted to achieve something really soothing, so I blended hibiscus (which eases sore throat) and rose petals with the calming red tea rooibos, known for its high vitamin and mineral content.

I used fully oxidized black tea from China for The Fashionable Dandy blend. I infused the tea with bergamot oil because I'm sure a fashionable dandy would wear a very pronounced cologne, and bergamot oil is in many men's (and women's) colognes and perfumes. It also serves as a flavor propellant, and I wanted this blend to be very forward, as a dandy would be.

But perhaps your very first tea, before you blend one named after a character or for someone you know and love well, should be a tea for you. Start with what you know you like. Do you like vanilla? Try this simple blend: get a few vanilla beans (expensive, I know, but potent!), and experiment. Scrape the seeds out of the pods (save the seeds) and steep each pod in a different quart of hot tea. I like black or oolong tea best with vanilla, but see what you think. Let the seeds and pods dry for a few days in a covered container, then try stirring a small amount of the seeds—just a tiny pinch should do—with about four tablespoons of, say, oolong tea leaves. The fragrance of the resulting brew is really heady, and the flavor is absolutely heavenly. Poke the dried pods into a canister of sugar to flavor the sugar.

When you are starting out making your own blends, it's important to begin by familiarizing yourself with as many of the teas, spices, herbs, and botanicals as you can, starting with what's easily available to you. Keep a tasting notebook to record your own personal reactions and associations with each ingredient. It's rather like learning about the world of wine, or the even wider world of cheeses: learning about tea and botanicals is a gradual process, but it's lots of fun, too, especially because, unlike learning about wine or cheese, you'll be creating your very own personal blends. Note what combinations you liked, and, perhaps most important, be sure to write down your recipes. Whether a mixture was a hit or a flop, you'll want to know how to recreate it or fix it for next time.

You can further familiarize yourself with the flavors inherent in different tea leaves by cooking with tea. As you will see in the final chapter of this book, tea really is one of the most versatile ingredients on the planet, and it can lend real dimension to your cooking. Try adding brewed black tea to turkey soup to broaden the flavor. Try poaching chicken in tea—amazing!— or using tea in your next marinade for beef or pork. Or try adding a good splash of citrus-infused vodka to a glass of iced tea to make a really refreshing cocktail. I think you'll be really surprised and delighted.

Getting Started

In general, black, oolong, green, and white teas all have different properties that make them special, and that should be kept in mind when you make your unique tea blends. Here are some simple practice tea blends, if you will, for you to try for each of these four types of tea as well as an herbal tea. These blends highlight the distinct qualities of the teas and will give you an idea of proportions for your own creations. You can halve them if you like or double them if you're making a bunch of gifts.

Anise-Chocolate Assam Tea

Assam tea is very bold and strong, so it blends well with milk to soften the flavor. The spices that stand up best to its flavors are star anise, cardamom, ginger, clove, black pepper, vanilla, chocolate, and cacao. Be brave—try mixing Assam tea leaves with your favorite curry powder, adding cayenne pepper if you like real heat.

8 ounces Assam tea leaves
½ teaspoon ground cardamom
½ teaspoon ground cloves
½ teaspoon cacao nibs
1 teaspoon finely chopped dried orange peel

Combine the tea leaves, cardamom, cloves, cacao, and orange peel in a 16-ounce glass jar with a tight-fitting lid. Cover and shake gently to combine well, then place in a dry, dark, cool place overnight. Use boiling water to brew the tea, and let steep for 4 to 5 minutes.

MAKES ENOUGH FOR ONE HUNDRED 6- TO 8-OUNCE CUPS

Lavender-Almond Black Tea

Black tea is the best blending tea for beginners, because its strong flavors make it the easiest to mix—you almost can't go wrong. Black tea leaves blend well with scented oils (especially rose and bergamot orange oils), lavender, dried lemon peel, peppermint, cassis, orange-tree flowers, chocolate, and almond.

8 ounces black tea leaves
2 tablespoons dried lavender blossoms
1 teaspoon almond extract
2 tablespoons ground toasted almonds

Combine the tea leaves, lavender blossoms, almond extract, and ground almonds in a 16-ounce glass jar with a tight-fitting lid. Cover and shake gently to combine, then set aside in a dry, dark, cool place overnight. Use boiling water to brew the tea, and let steep for 4 to 5 minutes.

MAKES ENOUGH FOR ONE HUNDRED 6- TO 8-OUNCE CUPS

Chai tea—redolent of warm spices, lightened with milk, and sweetened with honey or sugar—is especially popular these days. It is easy to blend at home, letting you play up your favorite components. Here are some chai tea blending ideas to help you get started.

Begin with an Assam black tea base flavored lightly with cinnamon, cardamom, and cloves. Blend a small amount, brew it for four minutes, and sniff and taste the tea very carefully. Adjust the cinnamon, cardamom, and cloves in your next batch according to your taste.

Try adding a little star anise, which is often used in traditional chai tea. Dried vanilla bean seeds are also a wonderful addition.

For refreshingly spicy chai tea, try adding black pepper, ground dried ginger, and cayenne pepper.

Delicious chocolate chai tea is easy to make: add cacao bits or even small pieces of chocolate to the chai blend. If you like, try adding ground almonds.

To make an exotic rose-scented chai tea, stir the blend with rose petals and droplets of rosewater. This blend is delicious hot or cold.

Chamomile Coconut White Tea

Pure white tea leaves are expensive, so to diminish the cost, make a half-and-half mixture of white and either green tea leaves or a mildly flavored herbal tea. White tea has such delicate flavor that you have to be careful not to overpower it. It blends well with ginger, vanilla, lemongrass, chamomile, lavender, passion fruit, peach, and coconut flakes. To make a wonderful Bellini, try iced white tea with pureed peach and chilled champagne.

8 ounces white tea leaves, or 4 ounces white and 4 ounces green tea leaves
2 tablespoons chamomile buds
1 teaspoon cacao bits
1 tablespoon dried unsweetened coconut flakes, lightly toasted

Combine the tea leaves, chamomile buds, cacao bits, and toasted coconut flakes in a 16-ounce glass jar with a tight-fitting lid. Cover and shake gently to combine. Set aside in a dry, dark, cool place overnight. Use boiling water that has cooled for a few minutes to brew the tea, and let steep for 2 to 3 minutes.

MAKES ENOUGH FOR ONE HUNDRED 6- TO 8-OUNCE CUPS

Orange Blossom–Vanilla Oolong Tea

Oolong tea combines the deep flavors of black tea with the grassy tang of green tea. It blends very well with flower petals and herbs and is strong enough to be used twice in brewing.

  8 ounces oolong tea leaves
  4 tablespoons dried orange blossoms
  1 vanilla bean, split lengthwise and scraped, pod and seeds dried overnight

In a 16-ounce glass jar with a tight-fitting lid, combine the tea leaves with the orange blossoms and dried vanilla seeds and pod. Shake well to combine, and store for 1 week in a dry, dark place. Use boiling water to brew the tea, and let steep for 2 to 3 minutes.

MAKES ENOUGH FOR ONE HUNDRED 6- TO 8-OUNCE CUPS

Mint-Ginger Chamomile Tea

Herbal teas can be every bit as refreshing as regular teas, even though they have no caffeine. The following tea is invigorating and soothing at the same time.

  5 sprigs fresh mint
  ¼ teaspoon freshly grated peeled ginger
  2 teaspoons chamomile leaves
  ½ teaspoon honey

Boil 1½ cups of water and then let it cool for a few minutes. Put the mint, ginger, and chamomile in a small teapot. Add the water and let steep for 2 to 3 minutes. Strain into a large cup and stir in the honey.

SERVES 1

Jasmine Green Tea

Green tea is famously grassy. I like to add something perfumed to cut the raw taste. Jasmine, apple bits, peppermint, and goji berries blend wonderfully with green tea. Try blending green tea with yerba maté for a quick surge of energy, or add a splash of green tea to hot or cold sake.

   8 ounces green tea leaves
   2 tablespoons dried jasmine blossoms
   1 tablespoon finely chopped dried lemon peel
   ½ teaspoon ground cloves

Combine the tea leaves, jasmine blossoms, lemon peel, and ground cloves in a 16-ounce glass jar with a tight-fitting lid. Cover and shake gently to combine thoroughly, then set aside in a dry, dark, cool place overnight. Use boiling water that has cooled for a few minutes to brew the tea, and let steep for 2 to 3 minutes.

MAKES ENOUGH FOR ONE HUNDRED 6- TO 8-OUNCE CUPS

Lemongrass
Rose Petal Red Tea

Red tea, or rooibos, is quite robust in flavor—herbal and fruity. As such, it blends well with fruits and flavorings such as hibiscus, rose petals, vanilla, lemongrass, cinnamon, berries, pomegranate, goji berries, and dried cranberries. It's also delicious iced with a good splash of rosewater.

8 ounces red tea leaves
2 tablespoons dried minced lemongrass
2 tablespoons dried rose petals
½ teaspoon ground cinnamon

Combine the tea leaves, lemongrass, rose petals, and cinnamon in a 16-ounce glass jar with a tight-fitting lid. Cover and shake gently to combine. Set aside in a dry, dark, cool place overnight. Use boiling water that has cooled for a few minutes to brew the tea, and let steep for 2 to 3 minutes.

MAKES ENOUGH FOR ONE HUNDRED 6- TO 8-OUNCE CUPS

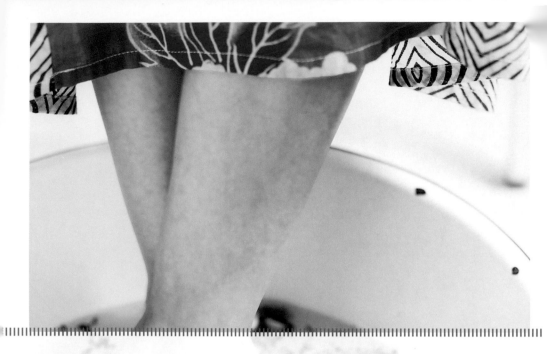

Tea for Health and Beauty

Sipping tea, a wonderfully relaxing and enjoyable pursuit all on its own, can have added benefits. In China and Japan, for many centuries, all varieties of tea have been used to promote good health and maintain vitality. Bathing in tea can help to keep skin detoxified, youthful, tight, and glowing. Hair, too, benefits from a tea rinse. Tea's salubrious and beauty-enhancing properties make it an indispensable part of any modern household, just as it has been for thousands of years in many cultures. When blending teas for health and beauty purposes, always remember to follow your nose, selecting ingredients with scents you enjoy most.

Multipurpose Cold-brewed Green Tea

Much of my beauty regimen at home revolves around one simple green-tea brew (though tea bags, which I do not recommend for making tea to drink, can also be useful). Green tea is rich in alpha-lipoic acid, the so-called eternal youth antioxidant. The compound helps to repair damaged skin cells and reduce wrinkles. It's often referred to as a provitamin because it can enhance the functions of other antioxidants. Alpha-lipoic acid also has the rare capability of improving skin from the inside out.

1 quart bottled water
3 ounces (½ cup) green tea leaves

Bring the water nearly to a boil, and remove from the heat. Brew the green tea leaves in the water for 15 minutes or longer. Strain the leaves and squeeze any remaining liquid into the brewed tea. Cool the liquid and then refrigerate it in a covered container. The brew will keep, refrigerated, for 8 to 10 days.

MAKES 1 QUART

For fatigued, puffy eyes or dark circles under the eyes, soak two cotton pads in the multipurpose tea, lie down, and place the cotton pads on your closed eyes. Rest with the pads on your lids for 10 minutes. (The same remedy also works with two cooled tea bags. If at all possible, use mint tea bags.)

To alleviate the sting of sunburn, soak a cotton cloth in the multipurpose tea and apply it to the sunburned skin. Leave it on the area for 15 minutes, or until the burned area feels cooler. Don't rinse. Repeat the treatment 2 to 4 times a day. After a long day of walking or standing, try soaking tired feet in the multipurpose tea for 20 minutes. The tannins in the brew will also kill bacteria that cause foot odors. For even further stimulating relief, try soaking your feet in a warm, strong peppermint tea brew.

Facial Care

If your facial skin is not overly sensitive, try mixing a teaspoon of very finely ground cornmeal with cooled brewed chamomile tea to form a gentle scrubbing mixture. Smear the mixture all over your face like a mask, let it dry, then gently rub it off and rinse. Your skin will be as smooth and tight as a drum.

If you want even more of an exfoliating treatment, try mixing powdered milk with chamomile tea to make a thick paste. Apply to your face, let it dry, then rub it off before washing your face as usual.

Tea is a natural astringent and rinsing your face with tea can be an effective treatment for blemishes. Don't rinse off the tea with water. For an even stronger astringent, try boiling ¼ cup water with 2 black tea bags. Let the mixture steep until it's cool. Remove the tea bags, squeezing out as much liquid as you can, and then add ¼ cup witch hazel to the brewed tea. Refrigerate, covered, for up to 10 days. Apply the brew to clean skin with a cotton pad as often as you like. Note that if you're light skinned and use black tea, your skin will be darkened—a natural tan without the threat of harmful (and drying) sun rays! If you don't want to darken your skin, just use green or white tea.

Hair Care

Tea has safe and effective coloration properties. If you have dark hair, you can use strong brewed black tea to rinse your hair to keep it dark and shiny. Chamomile tea will bring out highlights in your hair. And as mentioned above, you can give yourself a temporary "tan" by soaking your skin in black tea for about half an hour.

To strengthen and nourish your hair, try warming (without boiling) 2 teaspoons ground lavender buds and 2 heaping teaspoons peppermint tea in ½ cup extra-virgin olive oil. Let the mixture steep and cool for a few minutes while you dampen your hair, then massage the mixture into your scalp. Put on a tight shower cap to keep the mixture warm for 20 to 25 minutes, then shampoo your hair as usual, and rinse your scalp well. Repeat this treatment once a month, and you'll be surprised by how strong and healthy your hair will look and feel.

Oral Care

Green tea has been shown to improve gum health and help prevent tooth decay. Tea even makes an effective mouthwash. Try mixing peppermint tea with some anise seed or parsley seed for a wonderful and bracing breath freshener, or try the following recipe, which I use every morning. The exotic spice oils leave your mouth feeling clean and fresh for hours.

Chai Mouthwash

   2 drops clove oil
   2 drops cinnamon oil
   2 tablespoons good-quality vodka
1½ cups distilled water
 ½ cup brewed Chai tea

In a glass jar with a tight-fitting lid, combine the clove and cinnamon oils with the vodka. Add the water and tea and shake well. Keep refrigerated. Use as a mouthwash 1 tablespoon at a time.

MAKES 2 CUPS

Tracy's Special Tea Bath

I have saved sharing my very best beauty secret for last. As fully restorative as it is refreshing, a nice warm tea bath will melt away all the stresses of your day. Lower the bathroom lights, illuminate a few scented candles, and just let yourself drift. This is my favorite way to relax at the end of the day.

  1 cup coarse sea salt
  ¼ cup ground rolled oatmeal flakes
  ¼ cup powdered milk
  2 tablespoons black tea leaves
  1 tablespoon mint tea leaves
  2 drops geranium oil
  3 drops bergamot oil
  4 dried nasturtium petals, optional

Mix the ingredients well and transfer to 3 large tea sachets or tie up in 3 muslin or cheesecloth bags. Fill a standard tub with water at your preferred heat level and place 1 tea sachet into the water. Let the sachet soak for a few minutes before lowering yourself into the tub.

MAKES ENOUGH FOR 3 BATHS

Sweet and Savory
Tea Recipes

Tea's inexhaustible versatility is further demonstrated in these irresistible recipes, from tea-infused pound cake and tea cocktails to Green Tea Popcorn and Black Tea Fettuccine with Mushroom Cream Sauce. Teas and botanicals can really liven up familiar dishes and bring in unique flavors that in turn bring out the best in other ingredients. They can also make a healthful enhancement to many dishes. Some of these recipes flaunt a particular tea's distinctive flavor; in other recipes, tea helps to elicit the finer flavors in the dish, acting as a kind of flavor catalyst. For example, lapsang souchong tea imparts a marvelous natural smoky flavor to a variety of dishes. Black teas can provide quite a pronounced backstory in savory recipes. Believe me, once you start cooking with tea, you'll find dozens of ways to use it in your own everyday cooking.

Jasmine Tea Limeade

Jasmine green tea's floral, gently sweet flavors work so well with lime that I sometimes squeeze a quarter of a lime into a cup of jasmine tea, though the refreshing and easy limeade recipe, below, is by far my favorite way to enjoy the pairing. This summer drink is so popular, you might well want to double the quantities.

I like to serve this with ice cubes with pieces of lime frozen in them. To make the drink even more festive, you can make the lime ice cubes in fanciful ice cube trays, such as heart shapes or stars. Such trays are available at party stores and kitchen supply stores.

3 limes
1 12-ounce can frozen limeade concentrate, thawed
2 cups brewed jasmine green tea, chilled
2 teaspoons finely grated lime zest
3 tablespoons freshly squeezed lime juice
  Sugar

Slice 1 of the limes lengthwise into quarters. Reserve 1 quarter for serving. Slice the remaining limes crosswise into thin slivers. Add water to two ice cube trays and freeze for 1 hour, or until the liquid just begins to set. Push a lime slice into each cube and freeze overnight until solid.

Pour the thawed limeade into a pitcher. Add 3 cups cold water, the jasmine tea, lime zest, and lime juice and mix well.

Rub the rim of 4 serving glasses with the reserved lime wedge and invert into a plate of sugar to decorate the rims. Fill the glasses with the lime ice cubes and pour the tea limeade into the glasses. Serve immediately.

SERVES 4

Mo-Tea-To

This reimagining of the great mojito cocktail ups the ante of mint flavor by adding brewed mint tea to the mix. These are best made individually, crushing (muddling) the fresh mint directly in the serving glass.

    ¼ cup fresh mint leaves
    1 tablespoon sugar
       Juice of 1 lime
    ¼ cup brewed mint tea, chilled
    3 tablespoons light rum
       Crushed ice
       Soda water

In a tumbler, muddle the mint leaves with the sugar and lime juice, pressing them with a wooden spoon until the sugar is dissolved. Add the tea and rum. Fill the glass with crushed ice and add soda water to taste.

SERVES I

White Tea Sake

The delicate and velvety flavor of white tea works beautifully with sake. This could be served warm or chilled. Vanilla orchids are the only orchid with an edible blossom.

    ½-inch piece of fresh ginger, peeled
    ¼ cup brewed white tea, hot
    ½ cup sake, warm
    1 vanilla orchid, for garnish, optional

Steep the ginger in the hot white tea until the tea reaches room temperature, about 15 minutes. Pour the warm sake into a small teacup and strain in the white tea. Float the orchid blossom on top and serve.

SERVES 2

·· sweet and savory tea recipes ··

61

Green Tea Caipirinha

The caipirinha is an exotic and delicious drink that showcases Brazilian sugarcane liquor, cachaça. Mixing in green tea provides a little dimension to make the drink even more interesting.

½ lime
1 tablespoon sugar
½ cup brewed green tea, chilled
3 tablespoons cachaça
  Ice cubes

Quarter the lime half and drop the pieces into a tumbler. Add the sugar and then muddle the lime pieces by pressing them with a wooden spoon until the sugar is dissolved. Pour the tea and cachaça into the glass. Fill the glass with ice and serve.

SERVES 1

Black Tea Cognac

Chai tea takes the bite out of Cognac, creating a layered drink for postdinner sipping. The optional cream adds a delightful richness, smoothing matters even more.

¼ cup chai tea or chocolate chai tea
¼ cup good-quality Cognac
  Crushed ice
1 tablespoon heavy cream, optional
1 cinnamon stick

In a cocktail shaker, combine the tea, Cognac, and crushed ice. Shake well. Strain into a snifter or rocks glass. Stir in the cream, if desired, and serve garnished with a cinnamon stick.

SERVES 1

Mar-Tea-Ni

Vodka's mild grain-alcohol flavor benefits greatly from the addition of gently flavored green tea. Serve these before or after a meal or even as an accompaniment to sushi.

- 1 teaspoon chopped green tea leaves
- 1 tablespoon sugar
- ¼ cup good-quality vodka
- ¼ cup brewed green tea, chilled
- 1 cup chipped ice

On a small plate, combine the green tea leaves with the sugar. Moisten the rim of 1 martini glass with water and invert into the sugar mixture.

In a cocktail shaker, combine the vodka with the tea and ice. Shake well. Strain the martini into the sugar-rimmed glass and enjoy.

SERVES 1

Green Tea Popcorn

This is just great for movie night. Children love it, too, and it's actually a healthy treat, thanks to the antioxidants in green tea. If you and yours like spicy treats, sprinkle in a little cayenne. Grated Parmigiano-Reggiano also makes a nice addition. Whatever mix you decide on, do serve the popcorn in fun paper cones made by rolling 8½ x 11-inch sheets of white paper into cone shapes and taping the seams.

2 tablespoons canola oil
½ cup popcorn kernels
Olive oil
3 tablespoons chopped green tea leaves
Salt

Over high heat, heat a 3-quart heavy-bottomed pot with a lid. Add the canola oil, and when the oil slides easily across the bottom of the pot, add 3 popcorn kernels. When the kernels just start to pop, add the remaining half cup of kernels and cover the pot. Shake the pot constantly until you hear the popping stop, about 2 minutes. Transfer immediately to a large bowl, sprinkle with olive oil to taste, then toss the popcorn with the chopped tea leaves and salt to taste. Serve at once.

MAKES 5 CUPS

Green Tea and Watercress Tea Sandwich Pinwheels

Jasmine green tea lends a floral dimension to the classic teatime combination of cream cheese and watercress. The pinwheels are simply irresistible, and they work beautifully at high tea. White bread makes a delicate sandwich; if you like, substitute whole wheat bread for more flavor and color contrast.

>   One 8-ounce brick of cream cheese, softened
> 1 teaspoon jasmine green tea, chopped
> 1 cup chopped watercress leaves
>   Salt
> 4 slices soft, white sandwich bread, crusts removed

Combine the cream cheese with the jasmine green tea in a medium bowl. Toss the watercress with a good sprinkling of salt and then thoroughly combine the watercress and cream cheese.

Spread ¼ cup filling on each bread slice and, starting at the narrow end, roll up the slices. Wrap each roll in foil and chill for at least a few hours or overnight. Slice each roll crosswise into ½-inch-thick pinwheels, arrange the pinwheels on an attractive platter, and serve.

MAKES 24 SMALL TEA SANDWICHES

Black Tea Deviled Eggs

Black tea gives a surprisingly delicious, slightly dark edge to deviled eggs, adding sophistication to these perennial favorites. If the festivities call for it, these are even better topped with caviar.

  6 hard-cooked eggs, peeled and halved
  ¼ cup mayonnaise
  ½ teaspoon black tea leaves, chopped, plus more for garnish
  2 tablespoons minced onion
  1 tablespoon Dijon mustard
  ½ teaspoon white wine vinegar
     Dash of cayenne
     Chopped fresh flat-leaf parsley leaves, for garnish

Remove the yolks from the eggs (reserve the whites) and mash in a bowl with a fork. Stir in the mayonnaise, tea leaves, onion, mustard, vinegar, and cayenne. Spoon the mixture into the egg white cavities, or pipe the mixture, using a pastry bag fitted with a large star tip. Cover with plastic wrap and chill the eggs for 1 hour or overnight.

To serve, sprinkle the eggs with tea leaves and parsley.

MAKES 12 DEVILED EGG HALVES

Tea Eggs

These beautiful eggs are a lot of fun to make. Their mahogany-marbled exterior is created by cracking hard-cooked eggs and steeping them in tea leaves, sesame oil, soy sauce, cloves, and five-spice powder. They make a fine snack. Note that the eggs need to marinate overnight, so they should be prepared a day ahead.

6 large eggs
1 teaspoon toasted sesame oil
2 tablespoons dark soy sauce
2 teaspoons five-spice powder
6 whole cloves
2 tablespoons lapsang souchong tea leaves
  Onion salt

Put the eggs in a medium saucepan, add enough cold water to cover by 1 inch, and bring to a boil over medium heat. As soon as the water boils, turn off the heat, cover the pan, and set aside for 15 minutes.

Drain the eggs and rinse them with cold water. Tap them all over with the back of a spoon. The more cracks you have, the better the eggs will look. Return the cracked eggs to the pan and add enough cold water to cover by about 1 inch. Gently stir in the sesame oil, soy sauce, five-spice powder, cloves, and tea leaves. Bring to a boil, then remove from heat. Let the eggs cool in the tea mixture, then cover and transfer to the refrigerator. Let the eggs marinate overnight.

The next day, drain the eggs and wrap each one tightly with plastic wrap and leave them in their shells until ready to peel and eat. They'll keep for up to 1 week in the refrigerator.

MAKES 6 EGGS

Black Tea Fettuccine with Mushroom Cream Sauce

Cooking fettuccine in a light tea gives the toothsome pasta extra flavor and a wholesome color. Paired with earthy mushrooms and a rich, creamy sauce, the result is revelatory. For a smoky flavor, try making this with lapsang souchong tea leaves.

¼ cup black tea leaves, tied in cheesecloth
    Salt
1 pound dried fettuccine
4 tablespoons (½ stick) unsalted butter
8 ounces white mushrooms, sliced
1 cup heavy cream
1 clove garlic, pressed or minced
1½ cups freshly grated Parmigiano-Reggiano cheese

Bring 4 quarts of water to a boil in a medium pot, then turn off the heat and add the tea sachet. Let steep for 4 minutes. Remove the tea, season the water with salt, and return to a boil.

Cook the fettuccine in the tea water according to the package directions for al dente.

In a roomy skillet over medium-high heat, melt 2 tablespoons of the butter. Add the mushrooms and sauté until they give off, then reabsorb, their juices, 3 to 4 minutes. Scrape the mushrooms into a bowl.

Add the cream and the remaining 2 tablespoons of butter to the skillet and simmer for 5 minutes. Add the garlic and Parmigiano-Reggiano and whisk the mixture for 1 minute. Fold in the mushrooms and stir for 1 to 2 minutes.

Drain the pasta and return it to the pot over low heat. Add the mushroom sauce and toss until well coated.

Divide among 4 warmed bowls and serve immediately.

SERVES 4

White Tea– and Ginger-Marinated Chicken

The ginger slices and the ginger in the white tea blend give a nice zip to this sweet and tangy marinade. Serve with jasmine or basmati rice. Leftovers make the start of a great cold chicken salad.

½ cup brewed ginger white tea, cooled
½ cup soy sauce
½ cup duck sauce
¼ cup honey
    One 1-inch piece of fresh ginger, peeled and thinly sliced
6 boneless and skinless chicken breasts, butterflied and pounded to an even ¼-inch thickness
1 pinch chopped white tea leaves

In a medium saucepan, combine the brewed tea, soy sauce, duck sauce, and honey, and stir in the sliced ginger. Bring to a boil over medium heat, stirring occasionally. Let the sauce simmer for 1 minute, then remove from the heat, and let cool.

Put the chicken breasts in a large sealable plastic bag and pour the cooled marinade over them. Press out all the air from the bag, seal it, and marinate the chicken overnight in the refrigerator, turning the bag a few times.

Prepare a hot fire in a charcoal grill and lightly oil the grate, arranging it 4 to 6 inches from the coals. Place the chicken on the grate and grill, flipping once, for 3 minutes per side until it is nicely marked and cooked through.

Sprinkle the white tea leaves over the chicken and serve.

SERVES 6

"Barbecued" Pressure Cooker Country Ribs

The smokiness of lapsang souchong tea works wonders in recipes calling for a smoky flavor. If you don't like spicy food, omit the chile peppers and substitute 1 poblano pepper. Pressure cookers save a lot of time, and you won't believe how delicious and deeply flavored these ribs are—all in about an hour!

1 tablespoon peanut oil
4 pounds country pork (loin) ribs, cut into individual ribs
  Salt and freshly ground black pepper
1 medium yellow onion, chopped
2 garlic cloves, minced
¼ cup dry vermouth
1 cup ketchup
½ cup apricot preserves
1 tablespoon molasses
2 teaspoons Spanish smoked hot paprika
4 canned chipotle peppers in adobo sauce, minced,
  with 2 teaspoons of the sauce
2 habanero chiles, or more to taste, stemmed and minced
2 serrano chiles, stemmed and minced
¼ cup amontillado sherry
½ cup brewed lapsang souchong tea

In a 5- to 7-quart pressure cooker, heat the oil over medium-high heat. In batches, add the ribs and brown them lightly, searing each batch for 6 minutes total, turning once. Transfer the ribs to a plate and season them lightly with salt and pepper.

Pour out all but 1 tablespoon of the fat in the pot. Add the onion and garlic and cook until barely softened, about 1 minute. Pour in the vermouth and cook for 2 minutes, scraping up the browned bits from the bottom of the cooker, then stir in the ketchup, apricot preserves, molasses, paprika, chipotle peppers and sauce, habanero and serrano chiles, sherry, and tea. Stir well. Return the ribs to the pot.

Lock the lid in place and bring to high pressure over medium-high heat. Adjust the heat to maintain the pressure. Cook for 25 minutes. Remove from the heat and quick-release the pressure. Open the lid carefully. Transfer the ribs to a platter and cover with foil.

Position a rack about 6 inches from the broiler. Lightly oil a foil-lined cookie sheet.

While the broiler heats, bring the cooking liquid to a boil over high heat. Lower the heat to medium and cook, uncovered, stirring often, until the sauce is thickened and reduced to about 2 cups, 10 to 15 minutes.

Arrange the ribs on the prepared sheet. Brush with some sauce. Broil until glazed, about 2 minutes, watching carefully so they don't burn. Turn, brush with more sauce, and broil until the other side is glazed, about 2 minutes. Serve immediately, passing the remaining sauce at the table.

SERVES 4

Lion's Head Meatballs

The lemony notes in Ceylon tea give a nice boost to all the flavors in this luscious Shanghai-esque dish. The tofu makes the meatballs nice and spongy, and the napa cabbage rounds out the recipe to make a sumptuous one-dish meal.

For the Meatballs

1¼ pounds coarsely ground pork shoulder
    One 3-inch square of soft tofu (4 to 6 ounces), mashed well
1½ tablespoons sugar
1½ tablespoons soy sauce
  1 tablespoon hoisin sauce
  1 tablespoon unflavored Chinese rice wine or medium-dry sherry
  1 tablespoon grated fresh ginger
  ½ teaspoon ground mace
  ½ teaspoon ground cloves
  2 jalapeño chiles, stemmed, seeded, and minced
  1 tablespoon minced scallion, white and green parts
  1 teaspoon salt
  ½ teaspoon freshly ground white pepper
    Peanut oil, for frying the meatballs
  2 to 3 tablespoons cornstarch

For the Casserole

  1 small or ½ large head napa cabbage
1½ cups low-sodium chicken broth
  1 cup brewed Ceylon tea
  2 tablespoons soy sauce, or more to taste
  1 tablespoon unseasoned Chinese rice wine or medium-dry sherry
  2 teaspoons sugar, optional
  1 tablespoon cornstarch
  2 scallions, white and green parts, chopped

Make the meatballs: In a large bowl, combine the ground pork, tofu, sugar, soy sauce, hoisin sauce, rice wine, ginger, mace, cloves, jalapeños, scallion, salt, and pepper. Blend until well combined, but don't overwork the mixture. Shape the mixture into 8 large meatballs with wet hands, and place the meatballs on a sheet of waxed paper.

In a skillet large enough to hold the meatballs in a single layer without crowding, heat ½ inch of the oil over medium-high heat. Spread the cornstarch on a plate and lightly dust the meatballs. Brown the meatballs in the hot oil for about 3 minutes per side. Transfer to paper towels to drain.

Prepare the casserole: Remove the tough outer leaves from the cabbage and trim off about 1½ inches of the stem ends of the leaves. Cut the tender inner leaves in half lengthwise, then crosswise into strips, approximately 2½ inches wide. Measure 6 cups of the cabbage and save the rest for another use. Rinse the strips well, put them in a large microwave-safe bowl, and carefully microwave the strips for 15 to 20 seconds or until just warmed through. Alternatively, the strips can be steamed for 1 minute. Either way, refresh the strips under cold running water.

In a large glass measuring cup in the microwave or in a medium saucepan over medium heat, heat the chicken broth, tea, soy sauce, rice wine, and sugar, if needed, until the mixture simmers, about 3 minutes.

Meanwhile, arrange half the cabbage on the bottom of a 3-quart Dutch oven. Arrange the meatballs on the cabbage in one layer and cover with the remaining cabbage. Pour in the hot chicken broth mixture; it should barely cover the cabbage. Cook the meatballs over medium-low heat, partially covered, keeping the liquid at a bare simmer until the cabbage is just tender but not overcooked, 12 to 15 minutes.

Whisk together the cornstarch with 2 tablespoons water. Drizzle the cornstarch mixture into the pot and simmer, stirring gently, until the sauce thickens slightly, about 4 minutes. Garnish with the scallions, and serve.

SERVES 4

Rose Hip Jelly

The wonderful smooth honeylike texture of this jelly and the full rosy flavor make it ideal for spreading on toast, muffins, pancakes, and, of course, teatime scones. Try smearing the jelly on a little cream cheese spread on endive spears or celery stalks. This recipe can be halved, but because the jewel-colored jelly makes a nice gift, I like to keep one jar for myself and give the other away.

    6 cups filtered water
    8 cups dried rose hips
       One 57-gram package pectin crystals
    ½ cup lemon juice
    ½ cup brewed rose-scented tea
    5 cups sugar

Bring the water to a simmer in a large saucepan. Add the rose hips and simmer until soft, about 15 minutes. Remove from the heat and crush the rose hips with a potato masher. Squeeze the rose hips through 4 layers of cheesecloth over a large bowl, to make juice. You should have about 4 cups of rose hip juice.

Transfer the juice to a large saucepan. Add the pectin crystals, lemon juice, and the tea to the saucepan and bring to a boil over medium-high heat, stirring regularly. Stir in the sugar, return to a boil, and boil for 2 minutes, whisking constantly. Remove the pan from the heat and skim off any foam from the top of the jelly with a skimmer. Pour into 2 sterilized pint jars and seal the jars with rubber rings and caps. Let cool and then refrigerate. The jelly will keep in the refrigerator for 2 to 3 weeks.

MAKES 2 PINTS

Red Tea Applesauce

Piney-flavored red tea blends well with fruit, as this recipe deliciously demonstrates. Choose apples with just the sweetness you like. This recipe can easily be doubled.

  3 pounds apples, cored and cut into ½-inch-thick slices
  ½ cup apple cider
  1 tablespoon fresh lemon juice
  1 cinnamon stick
  2 tablespoons red tea leaves (rooibos), in a tea ball or tied in cheesecloth
  ¼ to ½ cup sugar or 4 to 6 tablespoons honey, to taste
  1 teaspoon ground ginger
  ½ teaspoon ground nutmeg

Put the apple slices, cider, lemon juice, cinnamon stick, and tea in a large heavy saucepan. Cover and simmer over low heat, stirring often, until the apples are tender but not mushy, about 20 minutes.

Stir in the sugar, ginger, and nutmeg. Cook, stirring, for 1 minute or until the sweetener is blended into the sauce. Discard the cinnamon stick and tea. Pass the mixture through a food mill to remove the skins, or process in a food processor until smooth. Serve warm or chilled. The applesauce will keep, covered in the refrigerator, for up to 1 week.

MAKES 3 TO 4 CUPS

Red Tea and Rose Petal Popsicles

These are even more refreshing and exotic than they sound! You can make the popsicles sweet simply by adding sugar to taste. Remember that once they're frozen, the popsicles will taste less sweet. Be sure to use fully organic rose petals, free of pesticides.

1½ tablespoons red tea leaves (rooibos)
¼ cup assorted organic fresh rose petals

Bring 3 cups cold water to a boil, then remove from the heat. Pour the hot water over the red tea leaves in a glass or ceramic teapot. Steep the tea for 5 minutes. Strain and let cool.

Meanwhile, divide the rose petals among 6 popsicle molds, filling them loosely. Pour the cooled tea into the molds. Freeze the popsicles for 30 minutes, then poke the popsicle holders or wooden popsicle sticks into the center of the nearly frozen popsicles, pulling up and down on the sticks to distribute the rose petals throughout each popsicle. Freeze until solid, at least 1 hour.

To unmold, run the outside of the popsicle mold under warm water.

MAKES 6 POPSICLES

Banana–Red Tea Sorbet

When the bananas develop speckles, transfer them to the refrigerator for a few days. Even if the skins turn black, the flesh of the bananas will work well in this recipe. The cold brewed red tea gives the sorbet a lightly piney and earthy flavor.

    4 medium overripe bananas
    ½ cup cold-brewed red tea
    ⅔ to ¾ cup sugar, to taste
    2 tablespoons fresh lemon juice
    1 tablespoon vodka

In a food processor, puree the bananas with the tea until very smooth. Pour into a large bowl. Add the sugar, lemon juice, and vodka and whisk to blend well. Cover the bowl and refrigerate until well chilled, at least 3 hours or overnight.

Whisk the mixture again. Freeze it in an ice cream machine following the manufacturer's instructions. Transfer to a quart-size container, cover tightly, and freeze for at least 2 hours before serving. The sorbet will keep for up to 2 weeks in the freezer.

MAKES ABOUT 3 CUPS

Jasmine Poached Pears with Matcha Tea Cream Sauce

The deep floral flavors of jasmine really bring out the best in the pears, which pick up a lovely richness from the cream sauce. This makes quite an elegant dessert!

  4 firm, ripe pears, preferably Bosc, peeled
  2 teaspoons light brown sugar
  ½ vanilla bean, split and scraped, or 1 teaspoon vanilla extract
  4 cups brewed jasmine green tea (use loose tea for the most flavor)
      Matcha Tea Cream Sauce (opposite)

Place the pears in a saucepan just large enough to hold them in one layer. Mix the sugar and vanilla seeds or extract with the green tea, stirring to dissolve the sugar. Pour the mixture over the pears, and turn the heat to medium high. Bring the poaching liquid just to a simmer, then lower the heat to maintain a very slow simmer. Poach the pears until they're tender but not mushy, about 10 minutes.

Let the pears cool to room temperature in the poaching liquid. Remove the pears from the liquid and serve dribbled with the matcha tea cream sauce.

SERVES 4

Matcha Tea Cream Sauce

6 tablespoons granulated sugar
1 teaspoon matcha green tea powder
4 tablespoons hot water
¾ cup heavy cream

Mix the sugar and matcha tea powder in a medium bowl. Add the hot water and stir to dissolve. Whisk in the heavy cream. Let cool to room temperature. The sauce can be covered and refrigerated for up to 3 days.

MAKES I CUP

Chai Tea Scones

What would afternoon tea be without scones? Putting chai tea and an extra boost of chai spices right in the scones makes dipping them in tea that much more delicious. If you like, add a handful of chocolate chips to the batter.

1¾ cups all-purpose flour, plus more if needed
  2 teaspoons baking powder
  ½ teaspoon salt
  1 tablespoon sugar
  1 tablespoon chopped chai tea leaves
  ½ teaspoon ground cinnamon
  ½ teaspoon ground cardamom
  4 tablespoons (½ stick) unsalted butter, chilled
  ¼ cup plus 1 tablespoon milk
  ½ cup orange juice concentrate, thawed
  2 teaspoons finely grated orange zest
  2 large eggs

Whisk together the flour, baking powder, salt, sugar, tea leaves, cinnamon, and cardamom in a large bowl. Cut in the cold butter with a fork or pastry blender until the mixture resembles coarse crumbs. Make a well in the center of the mixture, pour in the milk, and mix together with a rubber spatula until the dough forms into a sticky ball. Mix the orange juice concentrate and zest together and work into the dough. (Blend in a tablespoon or two of extra flour if the dough is too sticky to work with.) On a lightly floured surface, pat the dough into a 1-inch-thick circle, then wrap it in plastic, and refrigerate it for at least an hour or up to 1 day.

Heat the oven to 400 degrees and sprinkle a baking sheet lightly with flour.

Using a serrated knife, cut the dough into 12 wedges. Separate the wedges, spacing them evenly on the prepared baking sheet. Lightly beat the eggs in a small dish and brush over the wedges. Bake until the scones are golden on top and a tester or toothpick inserted into the center comes out clean, about 14 minutes.

Let the scones cool on the sheet for at least 5 minutes. Serve warm or at room temperature. The scones will keep in a tightly closed container for a few days, but they're best eaten freshly baked.

MAKES I DOZEN SCONES

Earl Grey Shortbread Cookies

These crumbly cookies are *made* for dunking into your favorite cup of Earl Grey tea. The tea leaves give the cookies an exotic flavor, and the aroma of the cookies baking is especially delightful.

- 2 cups (4 sticks) unsalted butter, at room temperature
- 1 cup packed light brown sugar
- 4½ cups all-purpose flour
- 1 tablespoon chopped Earl Grey tea leaves

Heat the oven to 325 degrees.

In a standing mixer fitted with the paddle attachment, beat the butter with the sugar until light and fluffy. Add 3 to 3¾ cups of the flour and the tea leaves. Mix well. Turn out the dough onto a counter sprinkled with some of the remaining flour. Sprinkle the dough with flour and knead for 5 minutes to soften. Roll the dough to ½-inch thickness and cut into 3 x 1-inch strips. Prick the dough with a fork to make rows of indentations, and transfer to an ungreased baking sheet.

Bake for 20 to 25 minutes, until the edges turn a light golden color—don't let the shortbread cookies darken. Let cool on a wire rack. The cookies will keep in a tightly covered container for 1 week.

MAKES 3 DOZEN SCONES

Mint Tea Cookies Dipped in Chocolate

Children especially love these. But adults will have a nostalgic reaction because the flavors in these refined cookies strongly resemble those of classic Girl Scout "Thin Mint" cookies. Adding mint tea leaves and extract gives the cookies additional mintiness, but not too much. After the batter is shaped into logs, it can be wrapped and frozen, then thawed and baked when desired.

    1 cup (2 sticks) unsalted butter, at room temperature
    1 cup sugar
    1 large egg
    ½ teaspoon mint tea leaves, chopped
    ½ teaspoon mint extract
 1¼ cups all-purpose flour, plus more for rolling
    ½ cup unsweetened cocoa powder
    ¼ teaspoon salt
       Six 1-ounce squares semisweet chocolate, finely chopped

In a standing mixer fitted with the paddle attachment, beat ½ cup of the butter until creamy. Add the sugar and beat until mixed well. Beat in the egg, mint tea leaves, and mint extract.

Sift the flour, cocoa powder, and salt into another bowl. Slowly add the flour mixture, half at a time, to the butter mixture, mixing slowly until well blended.

Divide the dough in half. On a lightly floured surface, roll the dough into two logs, each 1½ inches in diameter. Wrap each log in waxed paper and refrigerate for at least 5 hours.

Heat the oven to 350 degrees. Thirty minutes before baking, place both logs in the freezer for 30 minutes.

Slice each log into ¼-inch-thick pieces with your sharpest knife. Place on cookie sheets about 1½ inches apart. Bake for 10 to 12 minutes until the edges of the cookies are lightly browned. Cool on a wire rack.

In a double boiler or in the microwave, melt the remaining ½ cup butter with the chocolate pieces. Dip half of each cookie into the chocolate mixture and place on waxed paper for the chocolate to harden. The cookies will keep in a tightly covered container for 1 week.

MAKES 3 DOZEN COOKIES

Chocolate Chai Tea Cookies

These light and crumbly cookies will bring out all sorts of inner children! The spicy chai loose tea partners wonderfully with chocolate.

    1 cup (2 sticks) unsalted butter, at room temperature
    2 cups sugar
    2 large eggs
    ½ cup buttermilk
    1 teaspoon baking soda
    1 teaspoon vanilla extract
    1 tablespoon chopped chai tea
    ½ cup semisweet chocolate chips
    5 cups all-purpose flour

In a standing mixer fitted with the paddle attachment, beat the butter and sugar until creamy. Add the eggs one at a time, beating well and scraping down the edges of the bowl with a rubber spatula between additions. Add the buttermilk, baking soda, vanilla, tea, and chocolate chips and beat together slowly. When combined, add the flour, 1 cup at a time, and combine well. Cover the bowl and refrigerate the dough overnight.

The next day, heat the oven to 400 degrees. Lightly grease a cookie sheet.

Transfer the dough to a lightly floured surface. Roll the dough to ¼-inch thickness and, with a cookie cutter, cut half the dough into 2-inch rounds (or hearts) and place on the prepared cookie sheet. Bake just until the edges of the cookies are lightly browned, 7 to 8 minutes. Remove from the oven and let cool on a wire rack. Repeat with the remaining dough.

MAKES 4 DOZEN COOKIES

Lavender and Chamomile Crumb Cake

This is the kind of crumb cake you'd serve with coffee, but the flavors are combined especially for tea. Sprinkled over the finished cake, the yellow chamomile leaves and the lavender buds make a beautiful and quite flavorful combination. It's especially nice served a little warm.

2½ cups all-purpose flour
1½ cups packed light brown sugar
  9 tablespoons (1 stick plus 1 tablespoon) unsalted butter, chilled
  1 tablespoon plus 1 teaspoon chamomile tea leaves
  1 cup evaporated milk
  1 teaspoon baking soda
  3 teaspoons ground lavender buds
  1 cup coarsely chopped pecans

In a large bowl, combine the flour and brown sugar. Cut in 8 tablespoons of the butter using a fork or pastry blender until the mixture resembles coarse crumbs. Set aside 1 cup of the mixture for the topping.

In a small bowl, combine 1 tablespoon of the chamomile tea leaves with the evaporated milk and baking soda. Add to the flour mixture and combine well. Mix in 2 teaspoons of the lavender buds and ½ cup of the pecans.

Heat the oven to 350 degrees.

Pour the batter into a greased 8-inch square baking pan. Cut the remaining 1 tablespoon butter into the reserved flour topping, and stir in the remaining ½ cup pecans. Toss with the remaining teaspoon chamomile tea leaves and remaining teaspoon lavender buds. Sprinkle the topping over the batter and bake for 1 hour or until the middle of the cake is firm. Let the cake cool in the pan on a wire rack. The cake will keep, tightly wrapped in plastic, for 3 to 4 days.

To serve, cut the cake into squares in the pan and transfer to serving plates.

MAKES ONE 8-INCH SQUARE CAKE; SERVES 6 TO 8

Tea Lime Pie

If you can't find Key limes, don't worry. Frankly, I can't taste any difference between Key limes and regular limes in this recipe, which is all about the complementary flavors of green tea and tart lime.

  2 tablespoons finely grated lime zest
  5 large egg yolks
1¼ cups sweetened condensed milk
⅓ cup brewed green tea
½ cup strained fresh lime juice
 11 full graham crackers, processed to fine crumbs (1¼ cups)
  3 tablespoons sugar
  5 tablespoons unsalted butter, melted
¾ cup heavy cream

Whisk the zest and yolks in a medium bowl until the yolks are tinted light green, about 2 minutes. Beat in the condensed milk, green tea, and then the lime juice. Set the mixture aside at room temperature to let it thicken.

Adjust an oven rack to the center position and heat the oven to 325 degrees.

Mix the crumbs and sugar in a medium bowl. Add the butter and stir with a fork until well blended. Transfer the mixture to a 9-inch pie pan and press the crumbs over the bottom and up the sides of the pan to form an even crust. Bake until lightly browned and fragrant, about 15 minutes. Transfer the pan to a wire rack and cool to room temperature, about 20 minutes.

Pour the lime filling into the crust and bake until the center is set, yet wiggly when jiggled, 15 to 17 minutes. Cool to room temperature on a wire rack and then refrigerate until well chilled, at least 3 hours.

Up to 2 hours before serving, whip the cream until medium peaks form. Spread the whipped cream evenly over the pie with a rubber spatula. Return to the refrigerator.

To serve, slice the pie and transfer to serving plates.

MAKES ONE 9-INCH PIE; SERVES 8

Resources

Ingredients, teas, and tea supplies are available online through the following Web sites:

Dean & DeLuca
www.deandeluca.com
Gourmet ingredients of every stripe are available here, as well as a good selection of house-blended teas.

Formaggio Kitchen
www.formaggiokitchen.com
Artisanal cheeses, but also excellent chocolates and other prepared sweets, as well as Dammann Frères teas imported from France.

Gourmet Boutique
www.gourmetboutique.net
Caviar, chocolates, and a large array of loose and bagged teas.

Indian Foods Co.
www.indianfoodsco.com
Indian foods, spices, and teas.

Kalustyan's
www.kalustyans.com
A great resource for some of the most exotic ingredients, like lavender and rose petals, plus a good selection of teas.

Sur La Table
www.surlatable.com
Teapots and tea kettles, a full line of kitchen tools and cookware, and a good selection of teas and spices.

Persimmon Tree
www.persimmontree.net
Offers a good selection of loose teas.

The Tea House
www.the-teahouse.com
A highly informative site, with plenty of loose teas to offer.

Tracy Stern SALONTEA
www.tracystern.com
My entire line of SALONTEAS and BEAUTTEAS as well as a selection of tea brewing and serving products.

Williams-Sonoma
www.williams-sonoma.com
Teapots and tea kettles, a full line of kitchen tools and cookware, and a famous selection of prepared foods, as well as a good selection of teas and spices.

Acknowledgments

I give thanks to my family and friends for letting me cultivate the creative side of entertaining. I'm blessed to be nurtured within your circle.

I thank my adoring mom and dad for their continued love and support, and my amazing children, who were so proud of me writing this book. I admire all their creative input.

I'm most thankful for the best editor, Rica Allannic. You are in a league of your own! Thank you for your amazing professional guidance.

I am most grateful for the best literary agent, Michael Bourret. You have done a spectacular job and always continue to guide me in the best direction. Without you none of this is possible.

Tom Steele, thank you for working so closely with me and testing all the tea blends and recipes. I always looked forward to all your questions and inquiries and respect for the art of tea. You've been a dream to be around.

Thank you to all the fans of tea and my company SALONTEA. Special thanks to everyone who works closely with me. You have brought us to a higher level of excellence, helping to make tea a part of the everyday lifestyle.

I'm grateful to all the supporters, editors, television personalities, friends, press, and celebrities who love my teas and help to promote them. Thank you.

Enjoy life, drink tea, celebrate often.

Tracy Stern

Index